From the desktops of Andy and Gil Leaf

One of the most important lessons our father taught us is the value of reading. The exhilaration of turning a page and having words leap out, begging to be uttered and embraced, is a profound experience that is permanently etched in the mind. A book expands horizons, and from reading comes wisdom. This was his message to every child. A springboard for the imagination, a book can be educational *and* fun.

It is a huge joy that the key to the amusing, creative, and engaging world of our father can once again be found on bookshelves. He would be tremendously pleased and satisfied to know that today, more than seventy years and one century later, his words still have resonance—words that will be fondly remembered by generations past, and words that will be savored, chuckled over, and read countless times by a new generation of curious, inquisitive, and impressionable young eyes.

Your Name Here

HOW TO
SPEAK
POLITELY
AND
WHY

First published in the United States of America in 2005
by UNIVERSE PUBLISHING
A Division of Rizzoli International Publications, Inc.
300 Park Avenue South
New York, NY 10010
www.rizzoliusa.com

Originally published as *Grammar Can Be Fun*
© 1934 Munro Leaf

2006 2007 2008 2009 / 10 9 8 7 6 5 4 3 2

Printed in China

ISBN 10: 0-7893-1352-9

ISBN 13: 978-0-7893-1352-2

Library of Congress Catalog Control Number: 2005901423

Cover design: Headcase Design
www.headcasedesign.com

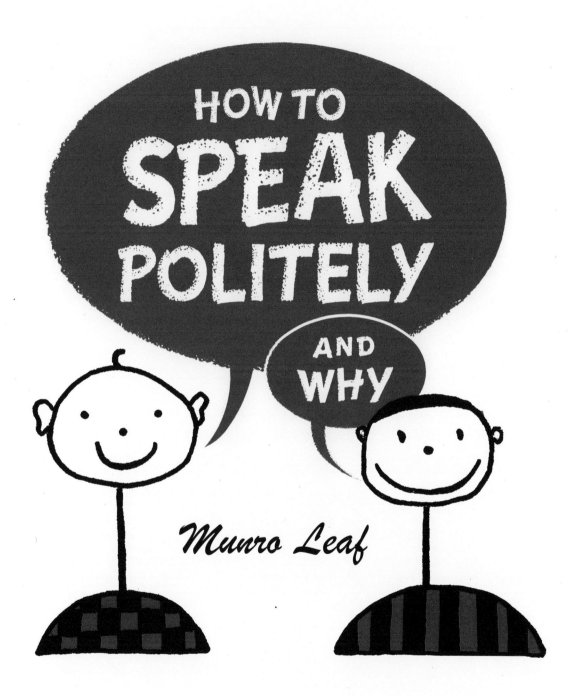

HOW TO SPEAK POLITELY

AND WHY

Munro Leaf

UNIVERSE

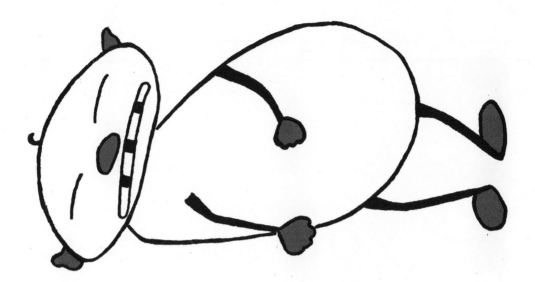

THIS IS AIN'T

Now you see why no one
even likes to hear his name.

Never say AIN'T.

That is being just as lazy as he is.

Say—

 I AM NOT

 YOU ARE NOT

HE or SHE  IS NOT

THEY  ARE NOT

4

THE WOBBLY NECKS

UH-HUH   UN-UN

Poor Wobbly Necks! They shake their heads and nod their heads and still no one knows what they want to say.

Some one says, "Would you
like to go?" and they shout
UH-HUH and UN-UN
then
Wiggle and Wiggle and Wiggle.

But no one knows
what they mean.

While—

YES   and   NO

Are always happy.

Everybody knows

what THEY mean

and

THEY don't have to

wiggle their

necks

at

all.

And this is one of the
most awful little
creatures of all.

YEAH

**PLEASE, LET'S NEVER
HEAR HIM AGAIN!**

This is
GIMME

Doesn't he look like a spider?

All day long he shouts
GIMME this, GIMME that
and grabs with all those hands.
If he should say
PLEASE GIVE ME
he would be much nicer and
he wouldn't look so odd.

GIMME has two little sisters
who are just as bad as he is.
They are

GONNA   and   WANNA

GONNA just
will not say
what she should,
which is

GOING TO

WANNA just
will not say
what she should,
which is

WANT TO

Don't YOU be
like

GONNA   GIMME   or   WANNA

G   Poor Old G

Don't you feel sorry for poor old G? He gets so lonely.

So many children leave him out when they talk about things that are fun—like

PLAYIN—

DANCIN—

RUNNIN—

FISHIN—

WHERE IS POOR G ?

Let's always take  along too.

PLAYIN •

DANCIN

RUNNIN

and
FISHIN

He has such a good time!

This is CAN

He is able to do things. That means he is old enough, or big enough, or strong enough to do them.

CAN

This is MAY

She is polite and asks when she wants to do things.

MAY

You would not say

Mother, CAN I have an apple?

Everybody knows that you
are old enough, and big
enough, and strong enough
to have an apple.

You mean to say

Mother, MAY I have an apple?

and

I

will

tell

you

a

secret.

If you say PLEASE when you say
MAY , you will probably get
what you want more quickly.

This is LY (say it LEE)

who likes action and movement of any kind.

If you walk or run, dance or sing, all of those take action. That is doing things and that is what LY likes.

So he comes along.

I walk slowLY 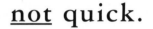   <u>not</u> slow.

I run quickLY   <u>not</u> quick.

I dance lightLY   <u>not</u> light.

I sing loudLY   <u>not</u> loud.

This is all about a very
messy creature and her
name is GOT.
Here she is.

And I'll tell you what she is.
She is a weed that grows
in sentences, if you don't
take care of them.

Good sentences are like
good gardens.

There is plenty of room for
the words that belong there
like

I HAVE A BALL

But—

When a messy word like  grows there, everything is jumbled.

In sentences

and
in gardens

so watch your sentences and

keep  away.

This  is NOT

Sometimes people say NOT

so quickly it is just N'T

like haveN'T

This  is NO

They are both nice, but

they should not get

together in the same

sentence.

They push and shove each

other—

just as they would if

they tried to sit in

the same chair.

This way.

I do NOT have NO books.

I doN'T want NO apple.

But—

If you let each one have
a sentence of his own,
it is fine, and they are
both happy.

I h a v e N O b o o k s.

I doN'T want an apple.

NOW

We shall go very

slowLY.

Everybody can DO THINGS

and

Everybody can HAVE THINGS

DONE TO HIM.

Now

When we DO THINGS

we are called

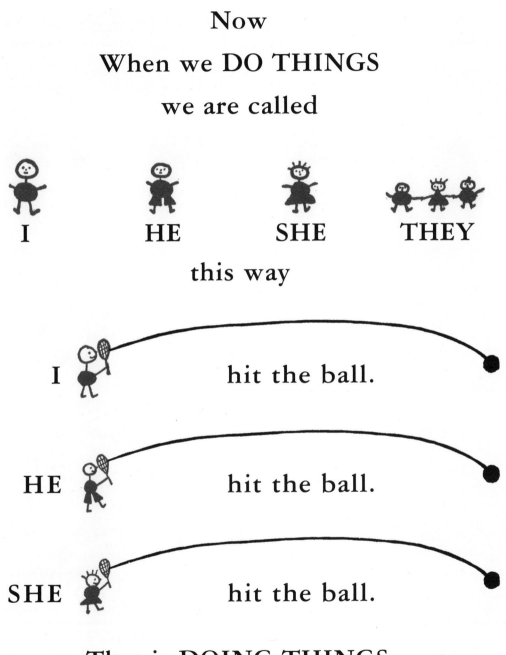

I   HE   SHE   THEY

this way

I   hit the ball.

HE   hit the ball.

SHE   hit the ball.

That is DOING THINGS.

When we HAVE THINGS DONE TO US
we are called

ME   HIM   HER   THEM

this way

The ball hit ME.

The ball hit HIM.

The ball hit HER.

That is HAVING THINGS DONE TO US.

Now think of us this way—
Are we DOING THINGS, or are
we HAVING THINGS DONE TO US?
and
you will always know which
we are called.

I   see   HER.

SHE   sees   ME.

HE   chased THEM.

THEY   chased HIM.

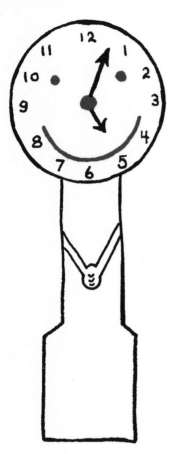

Do you know why old Mr. Clock and Mrs. Calendar are laughing so?

They are just waiting to see you all mixed up when you try to say the right

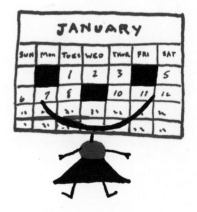

word for what happened at some other time.

You say now I SING.

That is easy.

But

If you did it yesterday,

WHAT do you say

And if you have finished

singing—WHAT do you

say

You should say

Now I SING.

 Some time ago

I SANG.

And if you have finished,

you say

I HAVE SUNG.

When I am thirsty

I DRINK WATER.

 Some time ago

I DRANK WATER

and when I have finished

I HAVE DRUNK WATER.

If I am hungry

        I EAT food.

 Some time ago

        I ATE FOOD

and when I have finished

I HAVE EATEN food.

If I look out of the window
        I SEE people.

 Some time ago
        I SAW people

and when I have finished

I HAVE SEEN people.

In the morning
    I GO to school.

Some time ago
    I WENT to school

and when I have finished
I HAVE GONE to school.

In school

      I DO math.

 Some time ago

      I DID math.

When I have finished

I HAVE DONE math.

DO is a word that mixes us up another way—that is, when we use it with NOT and say it quickly, DON'T.

We say

I DO NOT

or quickly I DON'T

and we say

YOU DO NOT

or quickly YOU DON'T.

But we say

HE   SHE

or

DOES NOT.

Never, Never

HE or SHE DON'T.

When I am sleepy

I LIE in bed.

 Some time ago

I LAY in bed.

When I have finished

I HAVE LAIN in bed.

If I have read my book
    I LAY it there.

 Some time ago
    I LAID it there.

When I have finished
I HAVE LAID it there.

Do those two get you mixed?

Well, remember that

IF you stretch yourself out	**IF** you put something else somewhere

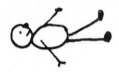

you LIE down. Some time ago you LAY down. And when finished you HAVE LAIN down.	you LAY it there. Some time ago you LAID it there. And when finished you HAVE LAID it there.

If someone says,

How do you feel?

You say

I feel WELL or ILL

not

I feel GOOD or BAD.

That is what you say if you mean that you behave yourself or are naughty.

And that is not what he wants to know.

THESE NEXT

PAGES HAVE

MISTAKES

I MAKE

AND

THE PICTURES

ARE DRAWN

BY